THE PISTILS

THE PISTILS

JANET CHARMAN

OTAGO UNIVERSITY PRESS
Te Whare Tā o Te Wānanga o Ōtākou

CONTENTS

high days and holy days

1. *Northland Panels*

winds drain to the horizon
tides
lap below the wrought-iron railing

here
we are sheltered in the hollow of the year
the hollow of the day

blowflies
loll and bang the afternoon to a close
the windows

nectarines
fuzz the trees
bach ghosts' disease

comes and
goes through this place
taking

everything
you'd like
to remember

the monarchs
rise
above

leaves
tūī
weave

soggy hills
slip their loads of red clay
into the bay

and move away

2. Xmas-New Year

chuck open the curtains
slap of sun
clothes sworn never to be worn again
put on
that nipple-revealing pocketless top
buttoned to the neck
these thrush egg blue pyjama pants
extra-large elasticated waist
extravagance
deranged lights pulled free of browned green tree
rubbish ornaments
find a respite with the League of Nations dolls
packed away on a case-by-case basis
Palestine Kashmir Timor Darfur Parihaka
rearrange the furniture so the kids
don't feature
eat up the fruit

3. *Anniversary Day*

don't pretend
you understand this celebration

Freud asked
Gawain explained

our fair
dominion

4. Waitangi Day

i. yes i do understand the principles of Te Tiriti o
    Waitangi
on the signing's one hundred and fiftieth anniversary
we climbed as many of the volcanic cones in Tāmaki
    Makaurau
as we could in a day
and i would also say
i have 'some knowledge of New Zealand's natural and
    cultural history'
to start we went up Maungakiekie
then Ōwairaka
which is really Te Wai o Raka if you read the legend on
    the lookout
which you can
since the vandals returned it
—one historian got it wrong
and all the others followed him
but tangata whenua assert
that it isn't named for the woman
swimming out
despite the cultural taboos
to rescue the drifting waka
that happened on the coast
in another place
although when i'm up there
i do think of her

ii. ascending Māngere mountain
was the last occasion
i remember changing a nappy
they're endless
you forget
but this one was cloth
i took it off

and scraped it with a bunch of kikuyu grass
which i buried in the earth
it was the only napkin i had left
refolded and pinned back
not conservation
desperation
then we kept climbing
up
to the view
it's funny how you recall
little things
i suppose i must have had the other baby
in the front pack
we never do know exactly what 'skilled use of
    knowledge'
will be required of us

5. *Picnic Days*

from wherever we were
she would get us
in the car
with a picnic
own crust apple pie or mince and veg
sometimes bacon and egg
a boiled potato sunk with butter
and eaten with black sand pepper
like sunset
food ingestion takes an instant
then in the shush of waves
forking beneath our feet
there is the icy current
making out
against our wriggling demurral
what we amount to
if we're a doable swallow

6. *Easter*

descend the avenue
the concert of leaf
an optical vee

sign bitters and spirit
a martini of sea
offered up to me

not dead
she invented
but risen

drink in the garden
raise the ocean
a *Mary Magdalene*

Brothers
why didn't we see it?

7. Wahine Day

A huge wave pushed the Wahine *off course and in line*
with Barrett Reef. The captain was unable to turn back.

Dad ferrying me to bible class
wind tries to get into the house
the front door doesn't want to shut it out
he makes it

heads bowed against the blast we plunge
through the sheltered garden to the hedged garage
in the dimness he lifts the plank from its carriers
loosed wind whacks the folding doors against the
    bumper
side on putting up the plank he escapes kneecapping

he shouts the weather is too strong
we brace ourselves against the car-shed doors to get
    them
in alignment and beat the living daylights back
he drops the plank into its sockets
retreating to the house the wind socks us

six tiles fly off the roof
the sinking news drips in
at Seatoun
a girl from school staggers up the beach on television
chains of water in her clothing

8. *Anzac Day*

dusted with poppy
these biscuits
to help you forget

9. *Matariki*

seven sisters
get up early
for a month or so
to go fishing

Taniwha
dreaming

10. Queen's Birthday

i. a short time
looking up at a crowd of women
stretching down
and around the corner
to The Coronation Film
for which my mother couldn't wait
the waiting taking too long
and tiresome for little children
which we were
we were promised we'd see the crown
and crown jewels
didn't we want to see those?
it was frock summer
i remember the woman behind us scorn
at my mother's dismay it would take so long
to get in
the woman's expression of disgust
that we were not robust enough
to wait
for as long as it took
and then my mother pulled us

ii. i ring my mum
and ask her if she wants to come for dinner
since it's a long weekend
and perhaps my sister
i have taken a chicken out of the freezer

11. *Parihaka Day: Guy Fawkes Night*

the last time
some lads of the village
set alight
the sentinel conifers
which made a fifty-foot blaze
either side of the churchyard gate
the Council had to chop them out

when our bonfire
gets going
neighbours call the authorities
but everything's under control
who'd arrest us?
we're atheists
and have the hoses
trained
on the margins
never relaxed till the flames die down
with the sirens

12. *Labour Day*

eight hours each
work play sleep

sometime
the other dead
you or i
will wake up in this bed

saying goodbye to the garden

Aunt
in curlers

takes
the daffodils

it caused me hassle
to purchase

cuts them loose
in a vase

Uncle
rapt in the front step light

while the woman
with the strong handshake

cleans
in their house

what can we give you?
they ask

a sherry
our single sheets

the picnic set
eight folding chairs

a kauri cabinet
surprised by borer

it was meant to last
forever

the path that winds down
to the lake

the magnolia in leaf
all the flowers over

the daphne odour
breathed in

something of times gone by
something of spring

i sit
on a wide red clay

brick they found
inside an old appliance

this
is what i want

and feel the sun
come down heavily on my skin

what way
does your new home face? i ask

east but we're not too fashed
about that

with the heater
on warm in the morning

or the afternoon
makes no nevermind to us

this
place

has sold
fortunately

and our new one
bought off the plan

is near
the dining room

but we don't
yet know

if there's a balcony
or a garden

'to speke of wo that is in mariage'

my darling
desires

to know me
better

I take her
to meet my mother

who has no reason
to remember

both of them
show the sweetest temper

as they speak
uncomprehendingly each to the other

my wife forgets to pretend and then
pretends to forget

no slouch

i dig out the couch
in the vegetable patch
which can't be for food crops
because we dumped a trailer-load of free sewage sludge
on it
that's full of heavy metals
now they tell us
so it's going to be a regimental rose bed

she made one
went out there when none of them would listen
and banged their heads together

loosed of claggy earth
see the underside of these sods
the shock of honey'd filaments

and now i rub this mote in my eye
with the back
of her wrist

when i was young

if no-one would pick us up
and it was hot
we'd jump in the Waikato
at Ngāruawāhia
and let the current take us

wasn't that dangerous?
what if it wouldn't let you out
at your stop?

the willows go right the way
down both banks
but at Huntly College
there's a bit of a beach
where we'd crawl ashore
and walk home wet

in your clothes?
how far was it?

about
from here to the dairy

did your mother notice?
what did she say?

i don't remember that

October garden

lying chilled
in the white blot of cherry blossom

visiting after the excision
Mum's gown strings open

a red pistil
threaded from her chest to a flask beside the bed

fill-in Grandmother making treacle tart
lattice work top fury

stop
playing

come
in

and find me
among the packets in the cupboard

the ginger
staring at her

Dad has to be the one
to put mercurochrome on school sores

a coarse green powder
dissolved in water to a deep staining red

at last
she is home

in her bra recommended to wear
a bag of birdseed

Mrs Valentine's instructions

the class divide
doppelgänger groups bob stove and cupboard
at six oxblood linoleum bench tops
lean and lift
bend and shift
a convenient height for the short fetch
i've become my partner's shadow
since after school she has to get the dinner on
do everything
knows to rock a chopping knife
peels thin
grasps the wooden spoon as if it's an old friend
that turns her into a machine for pounding
and she can't stop
till our ingredients
forsaking individual white and yellow
dissolve to the colour of the curtains
grease embracing crystal
a honeymoon couple
barely blush
time to crack into this pinkish slop
the transported egg
if it arrived from home unbroken
but i forgot to bring one and my friend is hacked off
despises my forgetfulness
accuses me of reading to excess
Mrs Valentine happens past
temper Girls
curdling is an unintended consequence
you must sift in reinforcements
strike to the heart of the batter by all means
but then draw back
with your spoon swoop gently round the margins

if you can keep your trapped air in
expect success
later in the heat will come the rising
my partner's heard enough
we scoop up the sweet nuts
dropped on a cold tray
our animus biscuits
not so close
yet not so far away

hometime

walk the swoop of Belt Road
in the dip at the creek
a moment when the pull is equally felt
between the gaping memorial gates of school
'Lest We Forget' you will be strapped if you need it
and the mother weighting at the top of the hill
her red roof tile her front windows
black blank shine
her white two-storeyed weatherboard authority of home time
—untangle the latch race the path
hunt through the house to find her where she sits
adrift in a novel
or conducting her day in some regimen of intellectual longing
with Freud and Jung in the sunroom
—on three sides light pulses in
Father Son and the Holy Ghost
summer on summer through glass the great gum nods
its foliage chewed by improbable green and indigo-bristle
    caterpillars
that emerged spotted orange from their nutty brown dwellings
Australians fat as your thumbs
finally the tree succumbs to her distaste for its messiness
leaf litter outside clutter stumped
—from one branch our brother's friend hung himself
until she sprang to cut him loose
boys and their nooses
cap guns skeletons he
was a sad one
—i kiss her
hear she's just sat down this minute
get milk bread and spread from the dark internal kitchen
mutton scent from a slow oven to reel in our father which art in
    garden

vegetables bubble now and at the hour of our dinner
—office leased he has us eat in radio silence for The News
flashes of plate banging met with growls
talk patters in after the bulletin urgent fret to get to the television
outside Belt Road sliding beyond its intersection with Saint Aubyn
past the residential housing where the foreshore rocks back up
to the kikuyu grass mattress of the hilltop
tides bob
the ocean sinks
we wash up

'look behind you!'

1.
in our church
there was no Mass
since Mum found Communion
tasteless
that meant the first theatre they took us to
was a Christmas panto
which took to us
every tier stuffed with kids
as if kids were all that matters
hanging off balconies
risking death in falls to the orchestra pit
you could not help but think of it
but on this occasion
we all chose
to postpone the indignity
hanging on to our gold-fringed
velvet-swagged boxes
with their hollow chocolate moulded fleurs-de-lys

driving back to Upper Hutt
some gender dissenting Methodist impulse
has me hunger for the minimalism of tights
and boy-chick boots to sing in with a switch
to get the lyric dot hopping
along that line
my sister wrote
starred and directed
a play for the neighbourhood
with my femme reasserted
as we fought over which of us
would wear Mum's
blue i'll-tell-you-why-when-you're-older lace
wedding dress with its panels of Madonna-crushed plush

who's grown out of this? we ask
she won and the show goes on—Madame Director
learning from Mum
plays her own heroine
in a renegade's virgin birth
—springs unbeknownst from a cardboard box
it was a triumph
the children in our terrace audience astounded
save the smarty pants
but Mum makes us give their collection money back
idiot
said their parents might resent it
offers them instead blood and flesh
raspberry cordial and shortbread

2.
then for Dad's Career
we shift here
to Taranaki

in the first month
we are summoned out of town
to Waitara
where we're given free
seats revealed to be
for guests of honour

who are we?

poi whirl
a night of karanga waiata action song haka
flaming satin shifts
lines of metrical piupiu
shudder into the world of light
drop dead gorgeous

a head school prefect
prances the aisle with a taiaha
he doesn't attack us
we live in New Plymouth

seated in the front row of the auditorium's
dress circle
Dad whispers into the blackout
'thank God we turned out'

but how did we turn out?

on The Voyage Home
to settle our excitement
the grown-ups rehearse the dying-language mantra
invoke the sanctified butter churn of Richmond Cottage
the First Ships
the Founding Families—none known to us
the inescapability of Redcoat Lane
the blood-drenched Huatoki Stream
drip drip
dripping
into our veins
the virgin-birth amnesia
as preordained

Telethon

and my mother-out-law
she's holding the fort
awake all night clasping her joyful bosom as the dollar total
 swings up and up
she won't tell you how much she's given
of her pension
because it makes her feel
minute by minute
like watching among her son's half-finished renovations
where the tiles are breaking
as the pipe's burst and the hot water's in flood
but now it hardly matters
since all of a sudden the little family has packed up
 and gone off to the old children's hospital
that they're fundraising to renew
with their week-old baby whose blood test says she has a life-
 threatening infection
and despite the lumbar puncture and a specialist assessment
the baby's father won't let them enter the room on the ward
 where they're supposed to be admitted
because it reeks to him of death
but i can't smell it
and when the nurse would force us from this ignorance
he shouts at her and pushes me and the little one into the
 corridor
that's our standoff right there
till her superior comes by sniffs and wrenches open the incubator
 doors
to pull out the flask of rancid formula
we gag
and then they insist we put the baby in the thing where she cries
 and i want her
back

and lean over and stick my breast through the box top opening
    for her to suck
her mouth reaches up
while the nurse looks at me as if i'm demented
some hillbilly who hasn't even invested in a nursing bra
and is not observing the decorum of the child's containment
anyway she says
it's for her own good
she won't want you she has an IV drip
full stop
now settle down
we just have to wait for the test results
both staying? we are
so they let us chuck the plastic covered mattresses on the floor
like we're on a noho marae without the pōwhiri and the kai
and we camp out there looking up to our daughter
nearly naked above us in her heated box
but perhaps it's the box heat giving her that temperature? he says
    and turns it down
do they know best?
with the tube of dextrose and antibiotics going into her arm
my rock-hard tits getting sore enough to make me septic
when i whine about it
to the night nurse she gets me a hand pump
sends me to stand in the shower and draw off all that surplus milk
    till i'm soft
oh yes very straightforward
but the light bulb has blown on the five-metre-high mausoleum
    ceiling
it's pitch black in there where the water runs cold for a first
    eternity over my flesh
but then
it does heat up
and i get some relief
slouching towards Bethlehem to find the night nurse leaving
the aide in charge while she and their one teenage patient zoom off

to The Town Hall Telecast
and she mentions their imminent departure to us
because we're the only adults within cooee
but if any of the several babies in the precinct were awake to it
they'd want to be hurtling off to get on TV too
and so what if it's three o'clock in the morning?
girls just want to have fun and forget they have cystic fibrosis and
    learn everything
about the stars and the gear changes between the Princess
    Mary Hospital and Queen
Street where parked on a yellow line the two of them dash
    through the swing doors
to the waiting applause of the studio audience
the phones are ringing for me and my gal bubbled up with a wild
    euphoria and
though the aide stays monitoring everything in the TV lounge
i don't want to watch any more
no i have better things to do like go and crash in the room with
    the allegedly sick baby
and her comatose father
where is it written that men shall sleep through anything?
and then i'm wallowing with them
poolside in the lounge bar of the hotel of sweaty metal fatigue
where your stitches ache and you wake up after a minute
to the cheery voice of the AM nurse dressed in shocking orange
    leggings
with her name in Fimo clay modelled with giraffe-style letters
    onto her child-friendly sky-blue hoody
and she tells us the blood tests taken before the infusion have all
    come back clear
what? nothing there
but just in case
they're finishing the antibiotics
and then our alternative healthcare organics-style Plunket nurse
    drops in
to say no matter what these orthodox practitioners think

it's the homeopathics she's been giving our baby that have done
    the trick
it is their feat
theirs alone
to have directed our little one home from the grey plain
and when the specialist comes along with his new house
    physician
we mention the distillation our darling is swallowing
and he tells the young man that 'you do get parents like this
but let them carry on with it since it's harmless'
and being parents like this
we do carry on with it
although now in the light of the scientific evidence
i don't know what to think about anybody's unorthodox hopes
    and practices
especially since seven years after
my mother-out-law has become vaguely aware
how little time she has left for heading up hill in love and trouble
and the medical profession can't offer her anything
though we don't know about that yet
because our daughter is off and running into her life at school
    and her sister
has grown and been born and nearly killed me
but that's another story
and this morning
who should come walking into the class i'm teaching at uni but
    the young woman who sped off to Telethon with that wiry
    ward charge yes
here she is
with portable oxygen and a head full of ideas and blue-black hair
    snapping eyes
and lips hungry for everything
that no night
or suffering
shall screen
burning up her hopes and dreams in a fire of living

rhymes for clitoris

red tendrils
enclosed
in snowy buds
break open
summer in a vase

the cat in clean wash
washes herself
when i stroke
grains of flea dirt
sift from her coat

motor running
she creaks
in a stretch
ragged fur now
and how thirsty she gets

our children come in
as the stars go out
last one home
forgets
to switch off the porch light

night shifts
my worries
—work you do yourself
but wouldn't wish
on anybody else

in daytime
the young keep to their beds
protect them

let their friends overwhelm them
the way you'd lick your own kittens

release
them
from jobs where
if you don't smile enough
the customer sends hate mail to your boss

not
war
make the drums they hear
`aiga
practising for Polyfest

see them adept
at ejecting lovers
who expect
sex
but have no rhymes for clitoris

selfie

used to be quicksilver
now when i pee
it's like drawing
deep conversation
out of me

notice my limbs
the lunar skin
spotted with the salt stains of torched summers

if i twist
there are dry chocolate ridges
i sometimes bite
in remembered sweetness

i do have these
nice suckling flabs o' breast

but years of trousers have walked away
with the hair on my legs

one tuft at the cleft
ornaments
the harbour of my hips

now for my hunch
that short story of my mother's horror
of her height
as i grew
i told it too

and on my face
this feeling mask i can't put off
though when my eyes read
our brain
denies
the long view of the right
and only accepts
the sharper counsel of the left

going west

there were the ones
young
and fit
who somehow got hit
by life's avalanche
and we
still gliding
over the snow
remember them now

hoping
to get
to whatever it is
our pursuit
finished

then more of the people we love
and some
of those we've only heard
vanish

Beth says
ok
so
it won't be finished
begin it

home confinement

for Aung San Suu Kyi

cut three
quince branches
poise them
in a glass vessel
alright a bottle
among the spoons
and knives and dishes
on the groaning table
thorn and bud
broken now
as sprouting
outer planks
pierce the plaster
answering branches
are moving in
my living space

a foliaged truss
binds the stove pipe
a tendril
insinuates
along the power line
where the electricity
knows
it's not forgotten

in these moist
interior rooms
leaves
in their warning flutters
remind me of books

to be set alight

gracious living

on her six-drawer
mirrored
oak dressing table
she installed muck-metal handles
because for all those years
she was offended
by the originals

plastic
they were
and shone like amber

so we won't keep it
i said
but now she's sent me
these knots
in my leg

she was so grateful
when my father
paid
to have hers
privately
untied

classroom

to fit our brains
this room as wide as tall
its windows fill with torn cream bun
when sluggish
after lunch
we want to fold our faces down on layered arms and
    fall asleep

a boy deployed
with a hook on a pole
to wrench the lofty panes
in cradle frames
agape
then cold tides rock us
engulf the archipelago of desks
in a sea of kauri planks

long division separates
no matter what we think of
those who can
and those who can't
all made to do the work

upon this floating hurt the teachers' walk
landing parables of mathematics
in chants
they have us carry the remainders in our heads

to spare the rod
thy staff
with bottled milk
shall comfort us

at intervals
drills complete
some may drift
to the horizon at the back of the room
becalmed
in heaps of tatty stories
Papa Babar sucks his pipe
all doings of the spectacled elephant obscured by cursive

and everything in Tintin foreign
masculine
save his think-bubble dog
who must
be a girl
look carefully
for her
a dress

day in day out
we march the halls with boys in shorts
unless
on message with another femme
once a term forgiven lessons
alone together voyaging the corridor
permitted the forbidden stair of the staffroom
where
we array the cups on saucers
by the elephantine teapots
plate the wine digestives from the tin tin

woe betide ye who forget
to switch on the boiling zip
for if their tea's not hot the teachers mope
then turn to chalk
and real work
billows from the blackboards

Standard One
comes with ink in wells
and warning lectures
we'll be strapped for waste or stain
yet know it in our squeaky pens
our blue-black veins
that ink is to tattoo
and cause explosions
none escape
the box canyon
the climb in colour-coded questions
through the painted sands of comprehension
where sentences are served
in weeks
and months
and years

here
only words
admitted
to make pictures
in thin air

on the high plateau
it's read or perish
but those of us who have the wax craft
break the cells open
find the honey
cram

the gold zipper

i put on the grey pants and the jersey with the gold zipper
this is toothpaste on the sleeve?
in one spit my best clothes are old

our bodies separate sexual pleasure
from penetration
so women have no need for contraception

men expect us to fuck
because it's what they want
—told as lyrical-operatic

clock there are no nerves in the vagina
the clitoris
is a substantial pelvic structure

and why is killing somebody of more literary significance
than a kiss?
because men say it is

i defy your authority
i won't ask for permission
O shut up and lie down here in this bed for a change and listen

our bodies separate sexual pleasure
from penetration
so women have no need for contraception

men expect us to fuck
because it's what they want
—told as lyrical-operatic

clock there are no nerves in the vagina

the clitoris
is a substantial pelvic structure

and why is killing somebody of more literary significance
than a kiss?
because men say it is

i defy your authority
i won't ask for permission
O shut up and lie down here in this bed for a change and listen

i put on the grey pants and the jersey with the gold zipper
this is toothpaste on the sleeve?
in one spit my best clothes are old

thirteen bystanders

1. there are suitcases in my room
full of old photographs
packed and ready to go
i never want to see them again

2. the men who came to do the concreting
ripped out all my father's boxing
he didn't know that with an elephant truck
full of slurry
our driveway could be trumpeted in one

3. my mother's engagement ring
with its four-diamond twinkle
on the deciding finger of her nurse
to keep it or take it to a fence
or keep it

4. spending my inheritance
on this flight
as the greenarse gasses
make life difficult for all of us
not in first class
unable to get up
or stretch

5. revisit my teacherly turn of the head
as i graded your story
and did not look back
at the stains on the sleeping bag

to see how they got there
and what you'd said

6. there are other ways to go
so please
let there be no nurse like me
who felt compelled
at that moment
to pinch the nose of the old dehydrated woman
the doctor said would die for refusing to drink
the junior—who was she? said *what
are you thinking?* and i stopped

7. when i'm tired
i look like my departed father
and now his late brother and sister visit
they say
in the apple orchard we were three
in the reading loft above the horses
in the farm kitchen
before you
before the war
before the bridge
we were three

8. on the death of my aunt's husband
we insisted
she must have a new bed
and fearful of the scorn of the men
who came to carry away the old mattress
i said they held the last of her married life
with its king size holes

9. the tangled extra blankets on our winter bed
once belonged to my aunt
they are thin but with the tint of egg yolk
and when we sent the rest of her old linens
to the vet to be cut up
for animal protection
i kept them

10. this morning walk
i saw a shag with a lure stuck in its throat
a skua circling
it makes me think of the girl aged three
taken off by a soldier and seen minutes later
in the arms of the commander
while at gun point her mother
was directed onto a bus
her child's creased photograph
shown to us in close-up
by the *Al Jazeera* journalist

11. for an eternity
when i was young
i only read books by men
now i've turned on them
the page i mean
and only read women
in the contents of journals
i assess for women's names
expecting the thud of feminine absence
while hoping
always
for an equal count
am i still missing out?

12. my mother is gone
but in death
laid straight
i noticed how always she was tall

13. the last time i spoke to my mum
she said
stay close
i might not be here next time you come

war memorial at Kohukohu

an arc of names
where the shock of brothers
is engraved with the dead

rain begins
pelting
down the jetty

sitting with the storm
in the passenger shelter
we each remember differently she said

—my uncle knew i was filming
but he wanted it
told

how
in front of him and his little sisters and brother
their mother was attacked

when the soldiers left
she would have drowned
if from the bank they hadn't begged

the river runs into the harbour
the tide
brings her back

daughters depart

they are in the waves
beating for shore
as the little fish of their absence
swim in the fissures of my long-grown bones

currents take hold
until
from sentiment i fall
to sediment

where the fumarole heat
escapes
in deep
dark
down
hair
a fontanelle
tells the stalker of memory
the necessity of tenderness

waste management

1. trash

well this is awkward
they've threatened to trespass me
from the Carl's Jr.
over the road
because i kept picking up the trash
from their business
which finds its way into the street
and i've been leaving it outside
their staff entrance
very irritating for them of course

today a staff member gripped my arm and said
this is not our stuff
we don't sell disposable nappies
then when she said trespassed
i was dumbfounded
all those petitions i sign
for prisoners of conscience
people rotting in jail for their beliefs

my terror knew no bounds
so now i don't pick up the trash
i just kick it from the kerb
to the middle of the road

2. *clean landfill*

getting in
before the rubbish men
come
the knowing flies
up to
something

early morning glitter
in the dark

beneath them
my clean recycling
where someone
has dumped a smile of butchered
chicken frames

purposeful corruption
buzzing gift

because desiring

to use your sacred taonga
and make new meanings

as in the gestational
when the unknown becoming infans
receives and takes
from their unknown becoming m/Other

yet she
as the originary source
retains completely
her own
subjectivity
while lowering
her ego boundaries
in compassionate hospitality

do you acknowledge this
as besidedness? that is
neither parasitic
nor symbiotic
and not colonising

welling

up from my bones
the light fractures through
the reviews
i've written
dance in my memory

little lapping waves
to inundate
the shoes of makers
whose texts
i've addressed
and assessed
in the dark inland towns
of my imagination
the large waves of the fire siren
call me out
in the middle of the night

to a gate between fields
where Papatūānuku
meets Hine Nui te Pō
they stand so close
in the whipping wind

i can't hear what they're saying
but as she speaks
Hine pushes the hair from her face
Papa bends at the waist
and laughs

what joke is this?

Ranginui

if ever i went after her
Rona would drench me from her tahā
though now and then
depending on the time of the month
she fills it with moonshine
and asks me in
once she said you're separated too
aren't you?
as if for her that made it better
Rona and my ex grew up together

our children i told her
blame themselves
but their mother and i
know it was more
too many too young
she always had her own plans
high five to that says Rona

our boys have started sending me up
weird stuff
but amongst it there are usable fragments
i keep them in a black hole
an inassimilable vortex
that Rona refers to as *your shed*

the best of their junk
i can reconfigure
as a car
that drives away the light years
and orbit by orbit i am also working on Rona
to come with
or is she
working on me?

the children
if they notice my emptiness
will still have their mother
to fight over
or they can want me
and look out for us
but we won't be back

the holy ghost and the lost boys

that whakamā pākehā chick
in the 24/7 Wendy's
is always eating buttered toast
hot with her coat open
milky star patches showing
on a ballooning blue nightie
draped so nobody sees
quite what shape she's in
since her baby's been uplifted

e Kare we say
why did you let that happen?

those big men
with pink hats creased like cunts
took my little boy into their prayers
then they opened that fire door
and pushed me in here

meant to be
over it

Hine sits down in the booth beside her
old mates
if Mere but knew
they go way back

those were your brothers Kare
following your father's orders
but long before they left you here
we had another bro who decided he could live forever
by re-entering my tuhinga

also unasked
a process meant to usurp my voice
but in our story
for his impudence
i locked him out of existence

remembering
Tatahore cracks up
you're not alive here Mere he tweets
then that flirt Pīwakawaka spreads his feathers
interrupts
Mere he says
you're not dead

in besidedness

while we're here
let's be clear
that Te Rauparaha's *Ka Mate Ka Ora*
actually tells
the passionate truth of a woman's generative strength
our agency with respect to life and death

The House of the Talking Cat

in the Letters
James K Baxter tells a lover
he rapes his wife

at the time
what he does to Mrs Baxter
is perfectly legal

so when he makes his boast in writing
to the woman with whom he's having an affair
he flaunts the fact he's above the law

James K Baxter
sexually predated women
including very much younger ones

those penitential sonnets
written at Jerusalem
withhold his reasons for self-flagellation

so he can be taken
as publicly engaging
in acts of selfless martyrdom

some have responded
to his private crowing
with expressions of concerned regret

anticipating that as Hero-Genius
Jim's description of her will reduce Jacqui to a sexual
    object
and obliterate her talent

but my question is:
what would motivate any critic
to render themself complicit?

watch J C Sturm
at The Women's Gallery
reading

the story about an unknown m/Other w.a.i.t.i.n.g.
with her little children
for the arrival home of an abusive drunk

and read
Jacqui
extant

bra dollars

Bay of Plenty

tucked in
where the silken goodies go
and come from

though in this case
my right breast is all set
to be a flat line sewn flat

i waited into summer for my diagnosis
saw how a benign White Island
only became Whakaari
for the pākehā
after an eruption with deaths

we were there
but had remained ashore
and watched the boats storm back
shadowed in ash
the *Daily Issa* chosen by the algorithm was:

>*spring gale Mt Fuji*
>*even the Samurai*
>*blown down the slope*

at the St John's ambulance shop i gave twenty dollars
exorbitant pittance for a two-buck wooden frame
and in it put a picture of myself
standing alive
above my great-grandparents' graves
at Ormond

then we travelled on
around Tairāwhiti
the East Cape
a saturation of pōhutukawa
whero everywhere
what was i—ten?
the year my mother's breast was taken

adjacent island: Moutohorā
captured whale
intact
as yet

Tolaga Bay

i walk the restored wharf
where my mum was sole-charge midwife

its cracks strapped with treated timbers
that sea harm
will not perish

up the coast
at Tokomaru
their wharf has all but
succumbed

with the decking giving out
as the posts carry the weight of thin air

her voice and self
flung onto the sea wind
nothing
more

door tender

—etymological origin of 'clitoris', from the Greek
'kleitoris'

a trek through bush
arriving at the party breathless

climb onto the verandah
two chairs
one each side of the open door
sit there
with the music pumping
from the lit living room
down the empty hall

then who should step up?
out of the dark
a sparkler
a hum
as if with this starry fingering
the sinews of the self
are vibrating
all
at once

My Mister

nobody
to whom i've recommended my Korean crush
has responded like this
except you

but so wrongly
you presume the antagonists should become lovers
while i am entranced because the hero spends key scenes
vacuuming

i want to break free and i love Freddie Mercury
but when did we ever see a *man* hoovering?
and Harvey Kietel polishes his piano like it's a car
as for Michael Parekowhai—if he eva wants a date with
    Jane Mander
he'll need'a work a lot harder
than laminated black arums and pāua
meanwhile
in Seoul
my hero
and that scene where his friend's embrace
doesn't engage with the exploitative romantic narrative
to which the stars are tightly tied

it's a deep chest compression
that leaves him
wriggling
enticingly
in a web of unrealised possibility

of course scriptwriter Park Hae-Young
is a woman
who knows how a man gets

everything
that's coming to him

tip-toe kisses
Genius
sisters cleaning
sisters vomiting

but bros
here's the thing
Lee Ji-an is listening in
to you
for me
so before you put another foot wrong
let yourself be lame
and go pick up where you left off
see what if

political theatre at the Canal Road trees

here we are on the verge
of seeing
The Big Canal Road Trees
cut down

already sweet sixteen green curtains have fallen

still
there are thirty natives left
standing before us as a forest chorus

while the audience winds in
this long-running production
feel the blow
through all the tiers of the ngahere
giving up a near hundred-year-old groan

the curtain lifts
as the whirlwind starts up
and the birds fly away
it all sways
but should we?

try walking home
alone with the afternoon matinee chill
stiffening your spine

when we calculate the box office
say there is something else your chain
saw

tell your friends
there must be no slash
keep it off the beaches
enter the leaf storm of applause

watch where you're going

every dusk that dull shrub
the pittosporum
at the entry to the Veterinarian's
is rowdy with invisible birds
which get to sleep
fitted among its foliage

today when i pass
where the leaves a hop
bristled with nightly chirps
there is only a great table stump
around which a team is planting
spikes of prostrate rosemary into a barked garden

one of them tells me the shrub was felled
because behind it a homeless man
defecated
but every morning
after he flew out foraging
i had seen his clean bedding
stored
there

a day later
the low plastic barrier
inserted to stop loose bark
drifting onto the path
unravels beneath the feet of passers-by

a child falls over it
watch where you're going
his mother snaps
that's the second time you've done that

womb

you lower the drawbridge
and cross over as a refugee
from patriarchy

laden with hormone blockers you come
carrying endowments of silicone
bearing scalpels

yes and your desperation
to access all areas
—that too we know

living in the castle's shadow
as we do
how can we accommodate you?

in your distaste for the menses in flood
where will you be? your pitch
invulnerable to abortion—imperatively

you may say: *we made the baby float*
but to me that reads as the royal we
when truth be told the roiling is all in her: the m/Other

your breasts aren't in suckle
you don't gestate: your vagina is socially constructed
for him: to penetrate

y/our internalised lack
redacts the organ of exclusive eros: a clitoris
you don't proceed to hot-flash tempests

friend
in those moments when you aren't at home here
ask yourself if you've kept a spare key

what would it take?
for you to unlock the keep
and help

ignore repeated word: delete repeated word

the stack of my unsold books
hidden under a shawl of red:
a mourner's mirror

i always took books with me
on our trips
to stick into the inferno of tourist information
at airbnb's

now i have to leave them in chiller hospital waiting
    rooms
where the staff fear cross-contamination
and must sanitise away my dirty
dirty poems

if not for covid you could
could you? have been diagnosed sooner
and lived
that way lies full howling moon can
can kicking about sex
get me to sleep?
or is sex thought keeping me awake?

instead let's head every day
to the Canal Road trees where life goes on
so i do the covid app check-in and ask the police to too

one officer has her taser buckled to her chest well
well well an electrifiable breast
to warn us against civil disobedience

some of us are unmasked
and trespassed
they take our photographs

some of us are arrested
which is for you
the goal of chemo

in the developer's plan all
all save one of the rare
ninety-year-old canopy natives
are to be felled

i am 66 you are 71: what's next?
don't make me laugh

when meeting fact-finding officials
i meekly offer tea so they'll have sympathy

later our green leaders publicly excoriate me
for pushing in
in on their exclusive
save the endangered micro-forest site tour
and someone angrily claims i don't listen
listen when others are speaking

i would like to say to them: i do a lot of listening
i hear the virus
she is whispering her excuses
ignore this she sings: go home: i am coming in

all in good time i reply

lose wellness: then become homeless

this uncovered
covered
dirty poem
red
red to the end

things you'll never know about breakfast

you surveilled the microwave window
tracking our porridge to forestall a lava flow
but now i cook my oats in a deeper bowl
and can look away
know the rising shadow won't overflow

i watch Jamie Oliver
the people's chef
go to Switzerland on TV
researching Bircher muesli
since then
instead of your weeks' worth of stewed
refrigerated fruit
i grate one raw Grief apple daily
into my plate

for forty years
we ate at our table
looked at each other
and spoke
television was a no go
i only allowed the radio
but your dispersal has blown me
to mourning TV

perched on our respective couches
John Campbell Breakfast grilling
relishes unintended spilling

for me
a tea towel
necessary to mop up

clickety click

leaning in
to my dream of prostitution
choosing the garments of allure
for my first assignation
when the realisation comes
that one breast
might not be enough
and after all
i'm sixty-six

spare me dear reader
your knowing wink
that women's disfigurement
can be men's entertainment

screen set to night shift

over my words an apricot wash
telling me from 10pm to 7am
i am not made to be awake

crossing Akaroa harbour under red sail
afloat in the bowl of the spent volcano
—a giant's glass of pinot

i flew in to channel my great-
great-grandfather
the people trafficker

he changed his name from Burton to Condon
to escape prosecution
fled from Australia to Aotearoa

when i come to account for him
crowds are gathered at Okains Bay
for the waka arrival on Waitangi Day

voices in waiata
we pākehā mostly join in dumb humming
could i live to hear us all jump in singing?

then a frightening situation: did some rounded up
and forced to walk to the station for an unknown
    destination
start thankful for their comfortable shoes?

and great-great-grandfather Burton
was anyone he heard sing black-birded?
what shoes would they be wearing?

leaden art gallery feet but *Te Wheke: Pathways Across
   Oceania*
has this Niuean hiapo (artist unknown)
—that calls up Loujain al-Hathloul to give me a lift

we fought them for it
we were not given
the right to be visible in the public space

and once when someone censored a poem i wrote
as culturally unsafe there was raised in me
a hail-storm of oestrogen argument

i watch Carey Mulligan resisting in *The Dig*
and feel a dress with inverted pleats is to die for
but not more than i insist on deep-pocket pants

cunt

if the poem contains polemic
don't expect them to rate it
as a literary artifact

they also say using colours
devalues poetic description
as feminine

even the most egregious villain
is eventually forgotten
but trauma is transmissive

when the cat keeps you awake
be grateful
for her interest

if it's raining quietly at night
go outside
and give thanks

journalists reveal our NZ army's war crime
now tune in to the *Al Jazeera* exposé of the Australian
    army
murdering in Afghanistan

to dehumanise his victim
the soldier uses a repeatedly bleeped
single-syllable

any
woman
intuits it

day or night

a handful of light
seeps in
above the curtain

the men who come
want to
have it over

fluffed up in someone's arms
these kiwis
released on television

among the gulls
at Back Beach
what a to-do about an eel

how curious
my glasses
leave little to the imagination

we see them beach
mustn't mind
have a cigarette

very busy very busy now
plenty of rubbish piling up
someone else does it

a fire across the road
made a clear space
so late afternoon sun's thrown up on this wall

scientists say opinions form in thirty seconds
having to look
the part

if not
for money
what?

the pistils

before they burned
the library at Alexandria
contained nine volumes of Sappho's poems
a copy is thought to have existed in the Vatican
until the early Middle Ages
since one of the popes' Sapphics reveal
his familiarity
with a blue skin
the ocean
poured between us
your reach across the earth to switch my bedside lamp
i wake and walk about my cell turned on ask: how are you?
ok you reply a little bit broken hearted when all i've read's alight
lives arc you aren't too far off
i sleep for half an hour and thanks to fiction i'm awake all night
then let me say how once in the middle of every day
i wade the creek
where you lift my wet hair
my spine unreeling as you press
the iron on the marron silk
whose intricate
whose difficult embroidery in
creased to this
and this takes the leaves glabrous heat
into the surrounding colours
where a fiery mantle sits up so the whole garment's
picked out
shaken
worn folded
as you saw
or let my breast point out the way the day opens
in the body of my city

improving the human

like a flooded river
humans have to rise higher

to improve its development potential
he poisoned the arboretum on his Canal Road acquisition

an arc of tension
like a dog watches for a new direction like a river in a new course

humans need improving
so the police give her a beating she's never forgotten

while they queue for subsidised spectacles
he gets down on all fours to find his contact lens and she has the
    laser operation

she greases her breasts hoping to reduce her stretch marks
—this little human drinks as if his life depended on it

humans need improving
the way truffle oil takes this cassoulet to fragrance central

human lies in bed human hand positioned under neck
when he says what he does tears make themselves felt

you so far off and yet what you write i'm reading in my own
    language
as if somehow you were lost in this room

how we fall apart
—our breath

he sold everything he had to improve humanity
but not a lot of what he sold belonged to him

rain grain fruit milk meat
down the rift valley arguments start a long walk to the fire

this pole dance supposed to form around the genome
my improvements: the aerial the burial—all directed to draw you
　　close

at the centre of my house there is a dark table—friend
come sit at my table

Mangawhai

ninety-three years passed
the earth groaned and burst
the house collapsed

hard materials
soft materials
time elapsed

one fire on the beach you lit when i was nine
the blackened foil of buttered hot potatoes
the big log we leant against

my first time upon the Hokianga

Mrs Johnny Johnson handed me a tin
bail she said
or we'll go under

ah there were schnapper!
when Joy and i launched the clinker
that was my second time upon the Hokianga

my third time upon the Hokianga
Ropata George was perilous drunk
not what you'd expect from a doctor
but he had a lot on his plate

they make her stand naked

while the other actor
ignores her

well i looked
that's what she was there for

the sweet curves
the shaven hair
the melting going on as she talks

her words
her words

Landeal Newz!

1. sixty-six million acres of grass
   gravy
   peas
   spuds
   mint sauce
   xmas pud
   and custard

2. tomato salsa
   pita pockets
   hummus
   yoghurt
   coriander
   sabayon and
   chocolate bonbon
   acres taken sixty-two million

stamen: stawomen

1.
female
Jacobin
hummingbird juveniles
are known to fledge in
flashy
male-bird plumage

2.
by doing so they evade
the body slamming
and aggressive pecking
males direct
at any female
they compete with
for food

3.
sing your hearts out
human girls
and boys
fly sip mate nest
in whatever plumage you wish
but until you call out the body slamming
peckers
do not rest

NOTES

Some of these poems have previously appeared in: *Blackmail Press, Broadsheet, Fresh Ink, International Literary Quarterly, JAAM, Landfall, Lopdell House Newsletter, Manifesto, Mayhem, More Than a Roof, New Zealand Listener, Poetry Shelf, POETRY, Poetry New Zealand Yearbook, Te Mātātuhi Taranaki, Titirangi Poets Anthology* and *Trout*.

Beth Serjeant produced *going west* in 2012 as a limited-edition print.

Page 65: Max White, *Fenced Madonna*, St Mary's Churchyard, Avondale, 2020

Published by Otago University Press
Te Whare Tā o Te Wānanga o Ōtākou
533 Castle Street
Dunedin, New Zealand
university.press@otago.ac.nz
www.otago.ac.nz/press

First published 2022
Copyright © Janet Charman
The moral rights of the author have been asserted.

ISBN 978-1-99-004833-3

Published with the assistance of Creative New Zealand.

Editor: Lynley Edmeades
Cover: Getty Images

Printed in New Zealand by Ligare.